With great appreciation for the helpful suggestions from many professionals in various fields, this book is dedicated to the young children living in families where someone has a serious illness.

ISBN-13: 978-0-9620502-4-4
ISBN-10: 0-9620502-4-5

ADDITIONAL COPIES: For individual
copies send $9.95 plus applicable tax and

Distributed by
Compassion Books, Inc.
7036 State Hwy 80 South
Burnsville NC 28714
828-675-5909
www.compassionbooks.com

WOODLAND PRESS
99 WOODLAND CIRCLE
MINNEAPOLIS, MN 55424
(952) 926-2665

A FACILITATOR GUIDE is available
for $30.00 and includes additional
information for leading a structured
children's grief support group.
FACILITATOR TRAINING WORKSHOPS
are offered in Minneapolis, MN. Contact
Woodland Press for more information.

PRINTED IN THE U.S.A.

ADULT FAMILY MEMBERS CAN HELP CHILDREN

Learn as much as you can about the illness. Get information for children from the national organization or your local library to help children understand basic concepts of the illness.

Use correct medical terms. Don't over explain but be honest. Fears and fantasies are often worse than reality. Describe what the child can expect if visiting hospitals or nursing homes. Offer choices of phone calls, letters, drawings, etc. to visits.

Reassure children that nothing they did or didn't do caused the illness. Find time to give them love and attention.

Take care of yourself and find support to overcome personal fears and anxieties. Children model behavior and coping skills from the adults they live with.

Encourage communication. Don't assume lack of questions means lack of interest. Children are more likely to express themselves in art, play or actions than in words. Find time to observe them during these activities. Ask teachers & others for their observations. Share your own true feelings to help them understand their own.

Headaches, stomach aches and behavioral problems may be caused by repressed feelings. Provide healthy outlets for energy release and expression with creative and physical activities.

Feelings of abandonment, helplessness, despair, anxiety, apathy, anger, guilt and fear are common in a family with serious illness. Children often act them out aggressively when there are no healthy outlets. Anxiety may lead to hyperactivity and behavioral problems. Try to maintain as normal a routine as possible. Children need structure to feel secure during stressful times.

Children need to be involved in appropriate ways. If they try to assume caretaker roles, remember they need to grow up normally without being burdened with adult responsibilities.

Coping with illness, financial and personal needs may overwhelm the parent who is not ill. Children need increased support from grandparents, neighbors and friends. They need to grow up knowing there is someone to count on or they may become too independent and distrustful.

There is a significant correlation between duration of illness and a child's behavioral difficulties. Illness lasting more than a year requires more intervention because the family focus is on something other than the child. Learn what services are available for your situation and needs through hospitals, churches, schools, community agencies and professional counseling. Inform pediatrician about family problems.

Information About Illnesses

For more information about a specific illness, you can obtain basic information for children and additional resources from the following national organizations. If the disease you are dealing with is not listed, ask your physician for the address.

American Heart Association, Inc.
205 East 42nd Street
New York, NY 10017
(212) 661-5335

American Diabetes Association
1660 Duke
Alexandria, VA 22314
1-800-232-3472

Alzheimer's Disease and Related Disorders
Association, Inc.
360 North Michigan Avenue
Chicago, IL 60601

American Cancer Society
777 Third Avenue
New York, NY 10036

American Lung Association
1740 Broadway
New York, NY 10019
(212) 315-8700

The Arthritis Foundation
115 East 18th Street
New York, NY 10003
(212) 477-8700

Assoc. For Care For Children's Health
7910 Woodmont Ave., Suite 300
Bethesda, MD 20814

Cancer Care, Inc.
The National Cancer Foundation, Inc.
One Park Avenue
New York, NY 10016
(212) 221-3300

Epilepsy Foundation of America
4351 Garden City Drive
Landover, MD 20785

Lupis Foundation of America, Inc.
4 Research Place Suite 180
Rockville, MD 20850-3226

Multiple Sclerosis National Society
205 East 42nd Street
New York, NY 10017
(212) 986-3240

National Hospice Organization
1901 North Fort Myer Drive, Suite 902
Arlington, VA 22209
(703) 243-5900

National Kidney Foundation
2 Park Avenue
New York, NY 10016
(212) 889-2210

Stroke Foundation, Inc.
898 Park Avenue
New York, NY 10021
(212) 734-3461

ABOUT THIS BOOK

This book was created to help children understand and express feelings when someone in their family has a serious illness. Illness brings many family changes and feelings about those changes. When someone has a serious illness, the entire family is affected. Someone gets most of the attention. Someone may feel forgotten. Someone else may begin to do certain things to get their needs met. Someone may choose the role of a clown to replace sadness with laughter. Someone else may try to be perfect or fix everyone else's problems.

The family balance is upset and everyone makes changes to try to bring balance back. Everyone reacts differently to a serious illness in the way that works best for them to fit into the family. Family roles change. If the illness lasts a long time, the roles may continue as unhealthy adult behavior patterns.

The art process allows children to express symbolically thoughts, feelings and perceptions about themselves and others. They learn to recognize and express feelings common to family change. Conflicts can be resolved and self-esteem is increased while coping skills are developed.

Educational concepts are presented in six units to help children understand the illness and how to cope with the changes it brings. Additional books are suggested. Each child will need a small box of crayons to illustrate their book. Crayons are suggested because they are more effective than markers for expressing feelings. Older children may prefer colored pencils.

Ask children to draw any picture that comes to mind as they read the words on each page. Do not make suggestions. Trust the child to make decisions about what and when to draw. Encourage ideas and expressions rather than drawing ability. During difficult emotional times, children often regress and scribble, erase, cross-out, draw something unrelated or leave the page blank. This is all right. It is the beginning of finding a voice for un-speakable thoughts and feelings.

This book was designed using the art process to help children learn some basic concepts of serious illness and provide an opportunity to learn about and express related feelings. Misconceptions may be revealed, conflicts resolved and self-esteem increased while coping skills are developed. It can be used individually or with a group facilitated by a supportive adult educated to accept feelings and encourage communication. Weekly sessions of $1^1/_2$ hours are suggested for each of the six sessions but individual needs may vary. The following objectives are included in the text and can be stressed with additional reading from the suggested books. (Check your local library and book stores for titles relating to specific illnesses.)

I. CHANGING TIMES pages 1-6
>   Accept change as part of life
>   Identify family changes
>   Discover personal life changes
>   Recognize grief from loss and change

ADDITIONAL READING
>   From Egg To Bird, Marlene Reidel
>   Our Changing World, Ingrid Selberg

II. UNDERSTANDING SERIOUS ILLNESS p. 7-13
>   Define serious and other illness
>   Learn basic cause of illness
>   Identify body parts effected by illness
>   Assess understanding and misconceptions

ADDITIONAL READING
>   Your Body, Carol Arnold
>   Germs Make Me Sick, Melvin Berger

III. FEELINGS ABOUT FAMILY CHANGE p. 14-19
>   Recognize and name feelings
>   Learn that feelings are all O.K.
>   Discover defense masks
>   Identify feelings about family changes

ADDITIONAL READING
>   I Have Feelings, Terry Berger
>   Oh, I'm So Embarrassed, Anna Dickson

IV. DRAWING OUT DIFFICULT FEELINGS p. 20-24
>   Recognize effect of feelings on behavior
>   See family pattern of expressing feelings
>   Identify personal difficult feelings
>   Learn healthy ways to express feelings

ADDITIONAL READING
>   I Am Not A Crybaby, Norma Simon
>   The Angry Book (Temper Tantrum Turtle), E. Weiss

V. LIVING WELL WITH ILLNESS p. 25-30
>   Assess family coping skills
>   Recognize personal needs
>   Identify support resources
>   Learn healthy coping skills

ADDITIONAL READING
>   All Kinds Of Families, Norma Simon
>   The Man Of The House, Joan Fassler

VI. FEELING GOOD ABOUT ME p. 31-36
>   Learn that play is the work of childhood
>   Increase feelings of self-esteem
>   Celebrate family strengths
>   Express hopes and dreams

ADDITIONAL READINGS
>   Tonia The Tree, Sandy Styker
>   The Man Of The House, Joan Fassler

FOR CHILDREN

This is your book. You will make it special as you draw the pictures that come into your mind as you read the words on each page. There will never be another book just like yours.

This book was written to help you understand the many feelings children often have when someone in their family has a serious illness. You will learn more about that illness and how you feel about some changes in your life. When one person is sick it affects everyone in the family. Illness brings change. Change brings both losses and gains. It may not be easy to see any gains at first but there will be many feelings about losses.

Sometimes it's easier to draw feelings than it is to talk about them. As you read the words on each page, draw the picture that comes into your mind. Don't worry about how well you can draw or how the picture looks. Just use colors, shapes and lines to tell a story about the illness in your family and how you feel about it.

Begin with the first page and do the pages in order. Circle any words you don't understand. When you have done a few pages, stop and share your work with an adult who cares about you. Most children feel better after they talk about their pictures with someone.

I hope you will want to share your book with others in your family so they can learn about your feelings from illness and change too. You can all learn to live well together.

Change is a natural part of life. Change in nature is easy to see. (draw some changes)

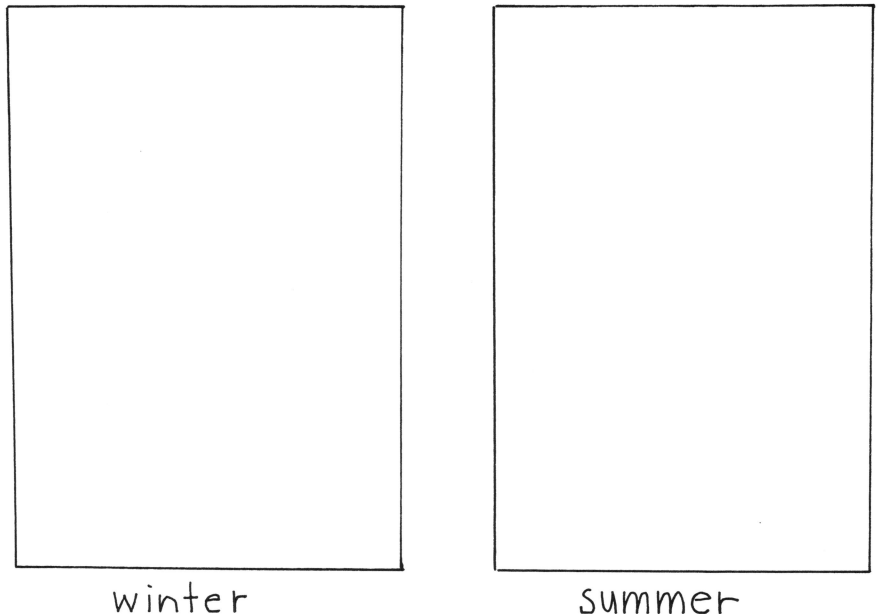

winter   summer

People change too!

Me ↗ when I was a <u>baby</u>
Living means growing and changing.

Me ... <u>now</u>

Change brings <u>gains</u> and <u>losses</u>. The <u>good</u> thing about getting older is...

The thing that <u>was</u> good about being a baby was...

It's O.K. to change and grow!

3.

Someone in my family has a serious illness.
There are some __BIG__ changes and some little changes.
(write them down. (Circle) the one that is hardest for you.
Draw a box around the one you like best.)

Serious illness affects everyone in the family.
It's O.K. to have problems. It's O.K. to talk about them.

4.

This is a picture of my family doing something fun together <u>before</u> the illness.

This is my family doing something fun together <u>after</u> someone got a serious illness.

6. Sometimes some things have to change.

This is a picture of the person with the illness.
(add the person's name)

He or she got sick because...

7.

The illness is called _____
and I __know__ these things about it...

These are things I __would like to ask__ about it...

8. You can __learn more__ from your doctor or books.

There are <u>many kinds of illness</u>.

Some are <u>simple</u> and people get well quickly.

Some are <u>chronic</u> and last a long time.

Some are <u>serious</u> and need special care.

Some are <u>congenital</u>. People are born with them.

Some are <u>contagious</u> and can be caught from others.

Some are <u>terminal</u> and bring death.

We need to learn more about illness!

9.

People get sick for many reasons. Germs called viruses or bacteria make people sick. They can travel from one person to another. Bacteria are very very small things. Some look like ° or ⌀ or ⌀ under a microscope. Viruses are even tinier and are all kinds of shapes. ✳ ⌀ ⌀ ⌀

Germs don't always make you sick. White blood cells in your blood kill most germs. These germ fighters are called the immune system. Sometimes it isn't strong and people get sick. Doctors can prescribe medicine to help the immune system kill germs.

The immune system can get confused and attack one's own body instead of infections and cause serious illness. Sometimes body cells don't work right and grow out of control and cause cancer. Doctors are trained to treat serious illness.

Illness may show <u>outside</u> the body like chicken pox.

Many illnesses do not show on the <u>outside</u> but affect the body <u>inside</u>.

Different illnesses affect different parts of the body.

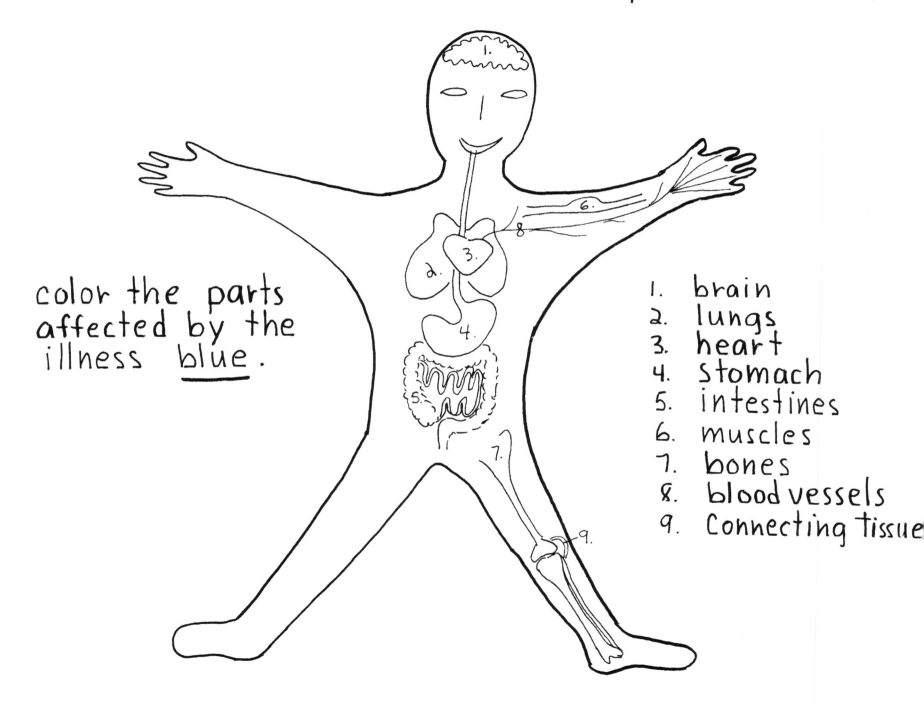

color the parts
affected by the
illness blue.

1. brain
2. lungs
3. heart
4. stomach
5. intestines
6. muscles
7. bones
8. blood vessels
9. connecting tissue

Some people with serious illness are treated at home with help from their doctor or medical team. Sometimes they may need to go to the hospital for special care.

Adults may be away from home more... or they may be tired more often.

Serious illness may bring many <u>feelings</u> about change.
The pain from loss and change is called <u>GRIEF</u>.

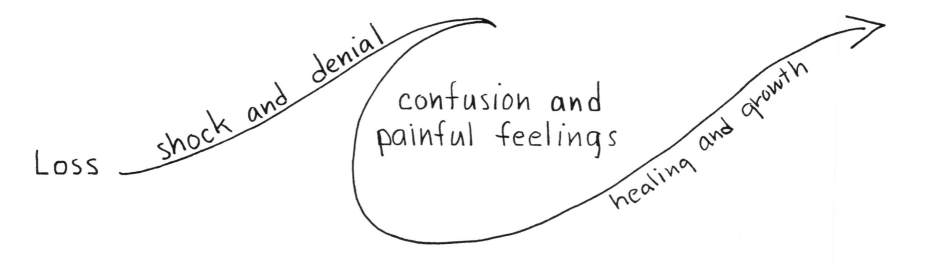

Loss — shock and denial — confusion and painful feelings — healing and growth

Grief comes and goes like
waves in the ocean. There
will be stormy times ......
There will be calm times...
Grief comes and goes.

There will be many feelings. Feelings may show on faces. (draw some feeling faces.)

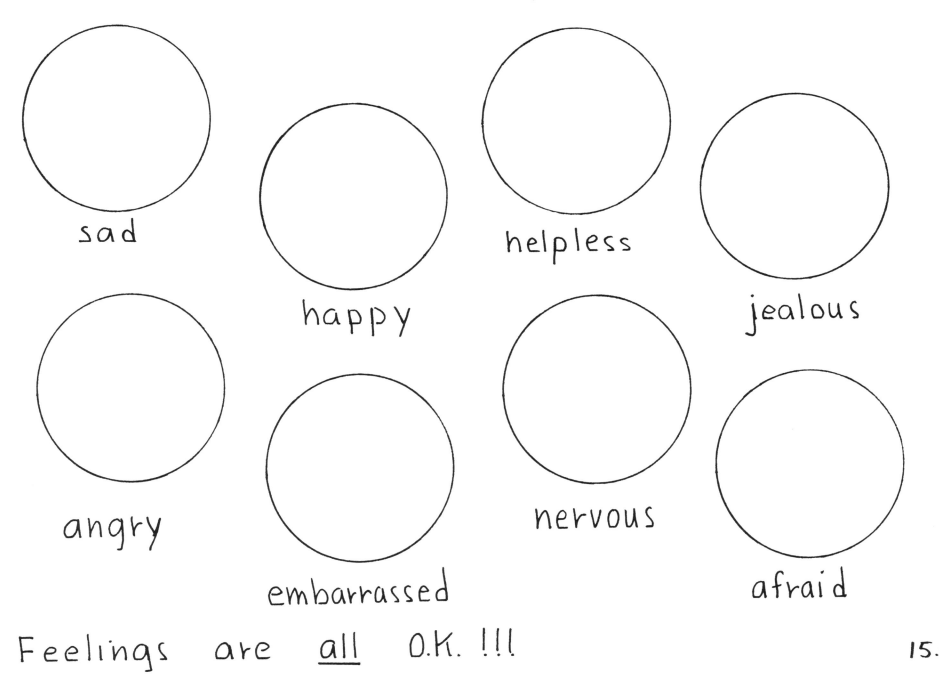

sad

happy

helpless

jealous

angry

embarrassed

nervous

afraid

Feelings are <u>all</u> O.K. !!!

15.

Sometimes people put on a "mask" to hide feelings they don't like to show.
(name and draw 3 feelings you sometimes hide)
with a different feeling

_____   _____   _____

Name and draw the "masks" you might use

feeling

_____   _____   _____

16.

Feelings are something you <u>feel in your body</u>

(color the places you
feel these feelings)

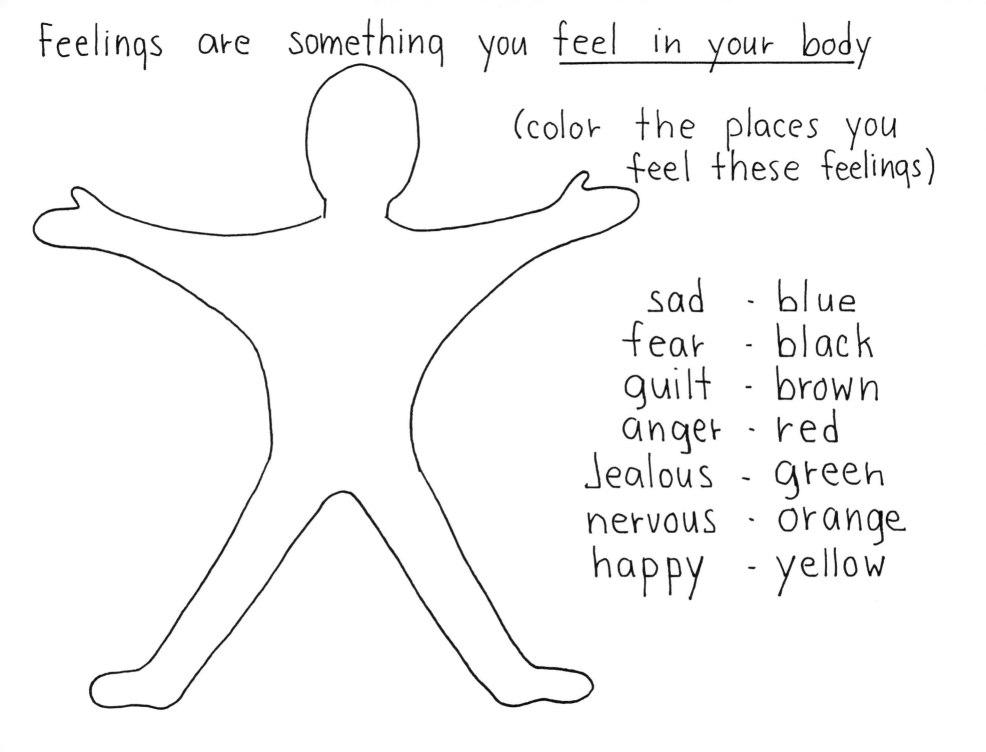

sad   - blue
fear   - black
guilt - brown
anger - red
Jealous - green
nervous - orange
happy - yellow

17.

If feelings are stuffed inside too long they may cause <u>aches</u> and <u>pains</u>.

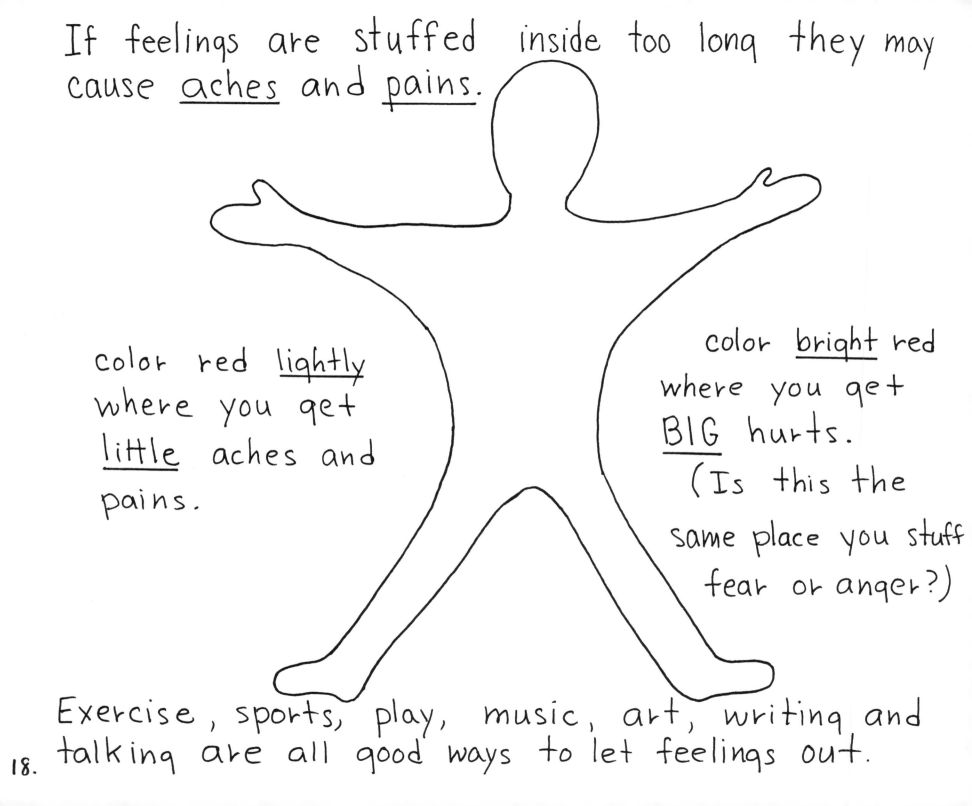

color red <u>lightly</u> where you get <u>little</u> aches and pains.

color <u>bright</u> red where you get <u>BIG</u> hurts. (Is this the same place you stuff fear or anger?)

Exercise, sports, play, music, art, writing and talking are all good ways to let feelings out.

18.

What do people in your family do when they feel...
    <u>Sad</u>   <u>Afraid</u>   <u>Angry</u>

Feelings affect the things you <u>do</u> or <u>say</u>.
<u>Everyone</u> feels sad, afraid and angry at times.

(Draw a picture to finish this sentence.)
I feel angry when...

When I feel angry I ...
(draw different kinds of things you might do.)

It's O.K. to feel angry but it isn't O.K. to hurt you, people or things. (cross out your ways that are not O.K.)

Sometimes I feel frightened...

When I feel frightened, I ...

22. Everyone feels frightened sometimes.

There are times I feel helpless...

Children <u>can't</u> <u>cause</u> or <u>fix</u> adult problems.

23.

Other times I just feel sad...

Crying is O.K. It lets the sadness out!

30.

Everyone in a family is affected by someone's serious illness. When someone is very sick the family may get out of balance. If one person gets most of the attention, others try new ways to get what they need or to bring balance. (Draw and name ways people in your family try to keep balance.)

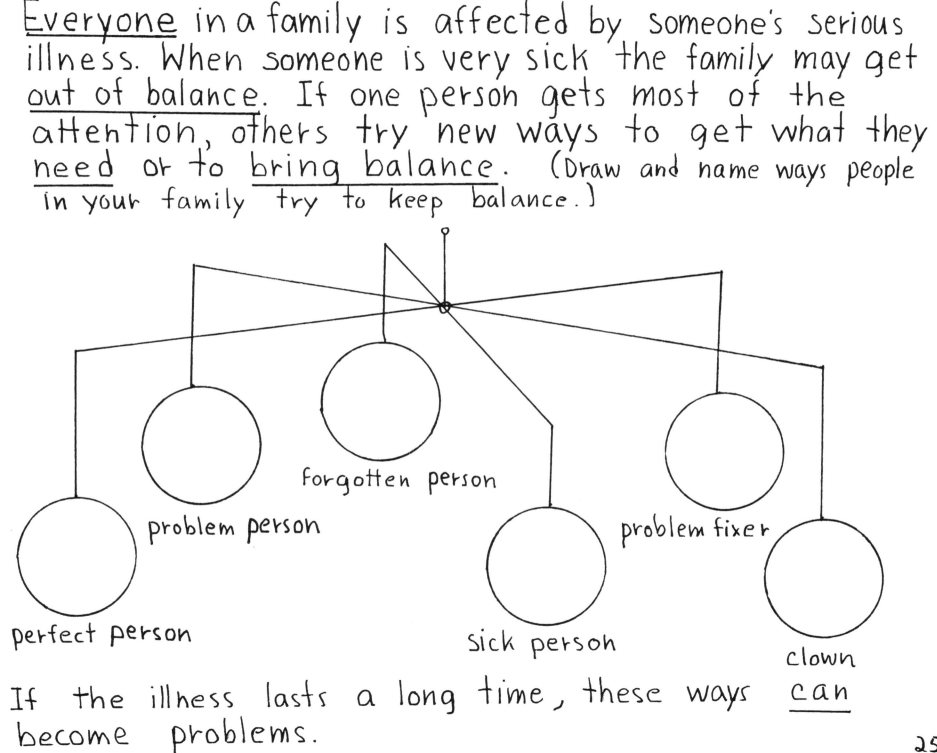

forgotten person

problem person

problem fixer

perfect person

sick person

clown

If the illness lasts a long time, these ways _can_ become problems.

Illness brings <u>stress.</u> (which demands more from the mind and body) You can learn healthy ways to <u>live with stress</u> when life is out of balance.

1. Eat healthy foods
2. Get plenty of rest
3. Get lots of exercise
4. Find support from others
5. Take care of yourself
6. Share the work
7. Find time for fun
8. Let feelings out in O.K. ways
9. Don't try to do what you can't do
10. Ask for help when you need it

Many people <u>care</u> about me and my family. We <u>need help</u> from others sometimes. (List names of people you can get help from and write the number in the "<u>support circle</u>".)

Support Circle

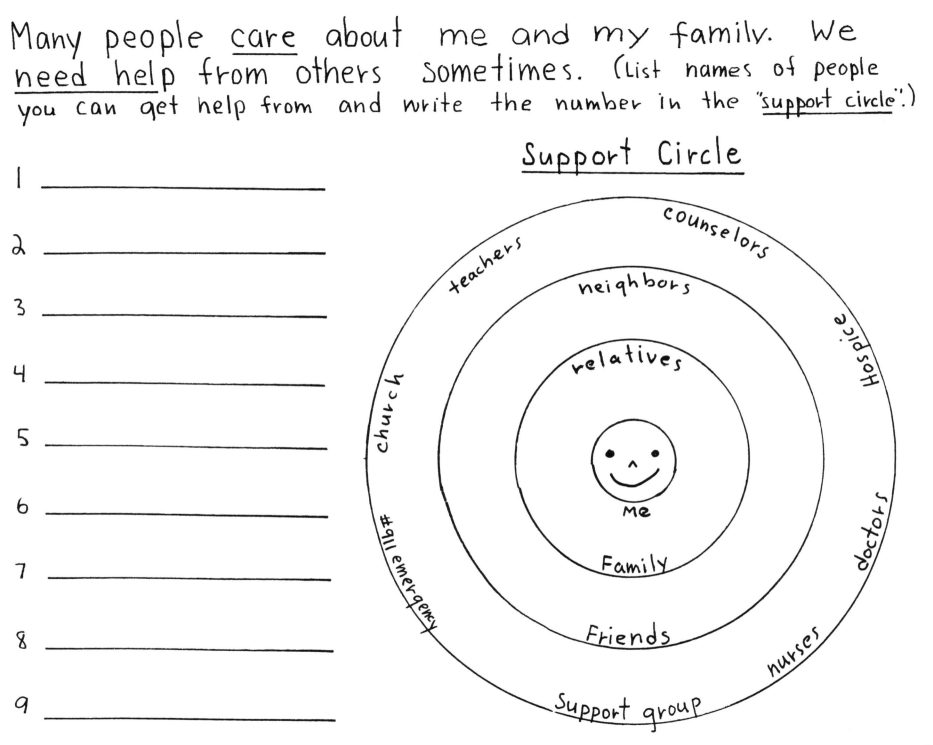

1 _____

2 _____

3 _____

4 _____

5 _____

6 _____

7 _____

8 _____

9 _____

My family is learning to live <u>well</u> together.

We get <u>exercise</u>

We eat <u>healthy</u> foods

We have <u>fun</u>

We <u>relax</u>

We keep <u>clean</u>

We get enough <u>sleep</u>

28.

There may be times when special people are gone or too busy and I feel <u>lonely</u>. I have a pet, stuffed animal or <u>something special</u> that will be there for me.

Everyone needs love and comfort.

Many people have God, a guardian angel or a higher power for support. Do you have someone?

30.

Sometimes I don't want to think about the illness. I just want to <u>play</u> and <u>have fun</u> with my friends.

It's O.K. to laugh and have fun. Play is the <u>work</u> of children even when someone else is sick. 31.

There are times I have <u>extra</u> work or things I <u>don't like</u> to do because of this illness.

Everyone has to help and it's <u>O.K.</u> to <u>not like</u> the extra work!

32.

My family is special. <u>Everyone</u> is good at something. (Draw your family and what is special about each one.)

No family is perfect. It is O.K. to be different.

I am special too. I am good at <u>many</u> things.

Unexpected <u>blessings</u> may come with problems and change. (can you think of something good you have gained?)

Growth comes from pain.

It's always good to have <u>hopes and dreams.</u>
I have a special <u>wish</u>...